Charles Larcom Graves

The Blarney Ballads

Charles Larcom Graves

The Blarney Ballads

ISBN/EAN: 9783744775939

Printed in Europe, USA, Canada, Australia, Japan

Cover: Foto ©Thomas Meinert / pixelio.de

More available books at **www.hansebooks.com**

THE

BLARNEY BALLADS

BY

CHARLES L. GRAVES

WITH ILLUSTRATIONS BY G. R. HALKETT

FOURTH EDITION

London

SWAN SONNENSCHEIN & CO

PATERNOSTER SQUARE

1893

PREFACE.

IN no more striking manner is the jealousy of the English manifested than by their reluctance to recognise the merits of Irish minstrelsy. In virtue doubtless of his long residence on English soil, Tom Moore has been admitted to the British lyrical Pantheon; but the claims of most of his compatriots have been steadily ignored. How many Saxon readers have heard of Buggy, the bard who so scathingly denounced *The Saxon Shilling* in verses of which *The Irish Tanner* is but a faint echo? Harkan, too, the author of *The Anti-Irish Irishman*; McGee, who sang of *The Irish Wife*; and McCann, who in inspiring strains bade his fellow Irishmen "strike for their country— O'Donnell Aboo,"—how lamentably few are their admirers on this side of the water!

The present volume has grown out of the desire to combat

and correct this ignorance. Just as De Nerval rendered
Goethe familiar in France by his paraphrases of Faust, so it
is to be hoped that through these ballads England may be
led to render tardy justice to the masterpieces from which
they have been humbly imitated. If the renderings appear
at times to be somewhat free, perhaps they will prove all
the easier reading on that account.

Nearly all departments of Irish poetry are here represented,
from the Bardic Ode to the Broadsheet. *The Arabian
Knight* closely follows the metre of Mangan's *Dark Rosaleen*,
in its turn a translation of a poem by an Irish bard of the
Elizabethan era. Specimens of Convivial and Humorous
Songs will be found in *The Promise-breaches*, based upon,
and in some parts borrowed from, *Purty Molly Brallaghan;*
in *Cave! to the Classes*, and in modernized versions of *The
Groves of Blarney, The Rakes of Mallow*, and *The Monks of
the Screw*. The street ballad is represented by *The Grand
Ould Man, The Wearing of the Blue*, and *Willy, I Hardly
Knew You;* while a chord of tenderer sentiment is struck in
such pieces as *Billy Machree*,—adapted from Gerald Griffin's
Gille Machree,—The Munster Maid, A Leap-Year Match,
and *Waiting for the Tide;* the last mentioned being closely
modelled on D. F. McCarthy's *Waiting for the May*. The
originals of other pieces will be familiar to readers of Moore
and Sheridan. Purists may resent such procedure as sacri-
legious in the extreme; but if it prompts them to consult
the Celtic exemplars, the end will have justified the somewhat questionable means adopted. Some few of these
ballads may lay claim to originality in form and sentiment;

but even here free recourse has been made to the Irish Nationalist Press in general, and *United Ireland* in particular, for metaphors, epithets, and expletives. To guard against any possible charge of plagiarism, it may be as well to state that the adjectives in *The Balpha-bet* are nine times out of ten borrowed from the source indicated above. The term "Tory Skunks" in *The Irish Tanner* is believed to be the invention of a Nationalist M.P. and true patriot.

In conclusion, grateful acknowledgment has to be made to the editors of *The Spectator*, *The Globe*, *The Saturday Review*, *The Scotsman*, *The Irish Times*, *The Union*, and *The Reflector*, for their courteous permission to reprint the pieces which originally appeared in their columns. These are, "The Streets of Dublin," "The New Guy Faux," "The Execration Ode," and "Oh, the Wild Charge He Made!" (*Spectator*); "The Arabian Knight," "The Green Above the Red," "The Anti-English Englishman," "The Wearing of the Blue," and "The Legacy" (*Globe*); "The Groves of Hawarden" (*Saturday Review*); "The Irish War Song,"—in a short and imperfect form—(*Scotsman*); "The Grand Ould Man" (*Irish Times*); "The Irish Tanner" (*Union*); "Cave! to the Classes," "The Irish Vote," and "The Balpha-bet" (*Reflector*).

" THERE is a stone there,
  That whoever kisses,
  Oh ! he never misses
    To grow eloquent :
  'Tis he may clamber
  To a lady's chamber,
  Or become a member
    Of Parliament.
  A clever spouter
  He'll sure turn out, or
  An out-and-outer
    To be let alone :
  Don't hope to hinder him,
  Or to bewilder him,
  Sure he's a pilgrim
    From the Blarney Stone."

CONTENTS.

LIST OF ILLUSTRATIONS.

BLARNEY BALLADS.

The Groves of Hawarden.

THE groves of Blarney aren't worth a farden,
  Whin the groves of Hawarden amazed I scan ;
And Blarney Castle can't one moment wrastle
  Wid the Gothic mansion of the Grand Ould Man.
There the shamrock and thistle together nestle,
  And ye'd fairly whistle at the fragrant leeks,
Or at Joseph Gillis, wid his Amaryllis,
  Gatherin' orange lilies in his Sunday breeks.

'Tis Misther Gladstone that controuls these regions,
  Like the Emperor Nayro or Pope Joan of Arc ;
Not even Pharaoh wid all his legions
  Could bombard that hayro from this princely park.
For the cute ould spider has Labbyrinths round him,
  Batin' Rosamund's bower itself to explore ;
And you're fairly addled whin you think you've cot him,
  To find he's shkedaddled by some fresh back door.

1

In these crooked courses he has grand resources
    For confabulations wid Government Whips ;
And open shpots to resayve deputations,
    Or to turn a pinny by the sale of chips.
And quiet corners for artful roguin',
    And sly colloguin' wid beau and belle :—
Professor Rogers and Mrs. Prodgers,
    Madame Pell-Mellikoff and Misther Parnell.

And after his speeches and fellin' of beeches,
    Shlippin' into knee-breeches and Irish frieze ;
He's off, the sly fox, like a modern Guy Faux,
    His Gaelic games for to organize.
On his pleasure-ground there he prepares for ructions
    By erecting obstructions from place to place ;
While Charles Stuart Parnell, wid skill infarnal,
    Arranges his three-legged obstacle-race.

He links Earl Granville to the martyr Mandeville,
    And Lord Herschell and Dillon ye'd see him yoke,
And Charlie Dawson to Sir Wilfrid Lawson,
    And Misther Bradlaugh to Archbishop Croke.
And Campbell-Tannerman and Docthor Bannerman
    He mixes up in his merry-go-round ;
And sets George Trevelyan riding postilion,
    In green and vermilion, for a million pound.

Ye'd see Butterscotch Rosebery playin' ould gooseberry
    Wid T. P. O'Connor and Proteus Blunt ;
And little Tim Healy, wid his toy shillelagh,
    Wid Earl Spencer startin' a Land League hunt.

And some of these athletes have stripped their coats off,
  And some have turned them upon their backs;
While Sir Patrick Ford and Sir Verdant Falstaff
  Bounce on stark naked in a brace of sacks.*

There's a saycret grotto, where two-headed Otto,
  That prize chameleon, in the dusk is found,
Wid Prince Krapotkin, and Misther Godkin,
  And Sir Edward Watkin, tunnellin' underground.
And there's a fishpond like the Slough of Deshpond,
  Wid slimy waters and throubled flood,
Full of Irish pikes and Sassenach leeches
  Fattenin' together in the emerald mud.

And there's an organ where ould Osborne Morgan
  Plays weddin' marches wid Morganatic grace,
Or sings *obbligato* to the *Moonlight* sonata
  In the most funayreal tones of his bass.
And there's Justin McCarthy and Prince Bonaparte,
  Sipping their caffy as they do abroad;
While silver-tongued Morley wid the lures of the Lorelcy
  Sings, "Come with me to Hawarden, my Maude, my
    Maude!"

---

* Lord Hartington, in his speech at Dublin on Nov. 29th, 1887, comparing Sir William Harcourt's utterances in 1873 with those delivered in 1887, remarked:—" Well, gentlemen, when we read passages in that character, I think the inquiry presses itself upon us, why it should be necessary, if a politician turns his coat, that he should divest himself of every particle of raiment which he ever possessed."

There's statues standin' at points commandin'
    Of ivery landin', to enslave the view ;
There's Matthew Harris, in plaster of Paris,
    Wid Pontius Pilate and O'Donnell Aboo !
And there's a picture, beyant all stricture,
    —'Twould make Raphael himself wid envy expire—
'Tis of William O'Brien, that Barbary Lion,
    Airin' his shirt by his dungeon fire.*

So now to take leave of this marvellous mansion,
    Which my poor scansion could never enshrine ;
But were I Horace, or Lewis Morris,
    Like any shoeblack I'd make it shine.

---

* " Doctor Moorhead visited Mr. O'Brien last Friday. .   . When Dr.
Moorhead visited the prisoner, he found him quietly airing his shirt at the
fire, it having just come in, nicely done up at the prison laundry."—*United
Ireland*, Dec. 10th, 1887.

"There's Matthew Harris, in plaster of Paris."

The Streets of Dublin.

(Originally sung at the Mansion House, Dublin, by MR. COLLEGE GREEN, *M.P., to the tune of* "MOLLY CAREW.")

[Not many years ago, the Corporation of Dublin hit upon the novel device of wasting time and irritating the loyal minority by rechristening the streets of Dublin. So long as they confined themselves to renaming bridges, nobody interfered; but when they pompously announced their intention of "making the names of the Dublin streets commemorative of important events in Irish Nationalist History," and when they went a step further, and by a resolution of the Council declared that in future Sackville Street should be known as O'Connell Street, the inhabitants thought it high time to assert their rights. A law-suit followed; and after the Corporation had wasted a great deal of their own precious time and of the ratepayers' precious money, an injunction was granted by the Court of Chancery, restraining the Corporation in their extravagant career.]

> LORD MAYOR and countrymen dear
>> Of this heart-broken Isle,
>> Just listen awhile;
> But first shut the window, bekase that it rains,
> And a shivering blast's blowing on to my brains.
>> Cripes! as long as I live,
>> I'll never forgive
> The tyrants for shaving my head.
>> My beautiful curls,
>> That charmed all the girls,
>> Ollagone! in the cell
>> Like martyrs ye fell

In the cause—Oh! it's passing the bounds of belief
To think they would treat an M.P. like a thief!
    No matther, some day
    For this same they shall pay :
Yes, I swear by the saints in the skies,
    Before the day's past,
    In terror aghast,
Their hairs on their heads will uprise.

The motion to move which I rise ;
    'Twill open their eyes,
    And it's this, and no lies—
To rechristen our statues, but not after Butt
Or Dan'l O'Connell. The likes of them, tut!
    Were Whigs in disguise
    Whom we Leaguers despise ;
For why ? They were squared most complete :
    But we, you might swear,
    Are harder to square
    Than a circle or globe,
    Or a barrel, be Jobe !
Already our principal streets we've disguised,
Our squares by the names of our martyrs baptized—
    As all Dublin agrees,
    Liffey's bridges and quays
By any name smell just as sweet.
    In the matter of smell,
    Plase God we'll excel,
Till the Divil's own nose we've surprised !—

But as for these statues, the scum!
    We'd like well to shatter 'em,
    Batter 'em, scatter 'em,
Tear 'em and tatter 'em, annihilate 'em,
Make a clane sweep, root and branch desoláte 'em.
    But whatever we feel,
    We must curb our zeal,
For we find it would take such a powdhering sum
    To drown in the say,
    Or remove them away,
    And fill up their places
    With our purty faces;
And the money's all wanted in Paris or London
To pay our expenses, or else we are undone.
    So we think, on reflection,
    There's not much objection
To laving them standing all plumb;
    And we'll not spoil the faytures
    Of the deaf and dumb craytures,
So long as they're not troublesome.

Now they're stuck up so high on a post
    That the Divil can't see
    If they're like you or me:
As for Nelson, that white-livered English poltroon,
Faith! his face might be meant for the man in the moon.
    Then why shouldn't his figure
    Betoken Joe Biggar?—
Joe Biggar, our pride and our boast!

And, bigger or smaller,
It's Biggar we'll call her;
And to clear up all doubt what the marble may mean,
We'll give him a coatee of beautiful green.
Lord! how he will curse!
The dead man changed at nurse!
Was the likes of that same ever seen?
Arrah! Nelson, "have at you!"—
If we don't raze your statue,
We'll go mighty nigh raising your ghost.

Let 'em talk of their interests vested!
Whigs and Tories may swear,
But what do we care?
Their heaviest losses we count for our gain—
And curses are music to those who disdain.
We'll show them no pity,
For Dublin's our city,
We may do what we like with our own.
No more we'll allow,
With a wreath on his brow,
That "souper *" King Will
The broad street to fill
With his carcase;—No, Davitt shall sit there of course,
Oh! 'tis he would look illigant sot on a horse,

---

* A contemptuous synonym for Protestant, originally applied to those whose conversion from Roman Catholicism was supposed to have been effected by gifts of soup.

Wid a stick in his hand,—
He'd look mighty grand,
And 'tis then he would show you his mettle,
With three legs in the air,
And his tail flowing fair,—
In his stirrups bold Davitt we'll settle.

And now, boys, before we conclude,
I propose that we do
Rechristen a few
Of our neighbours, who're men of notorious bad name.
Our landlords, the reptiles! we'll call 'em "Ground Game";
And then in all rayson,
They'd be iver in sayson,
And the tinants might pot 'em, when viewed;
While if licence they'd none
To carry a gun,
They'd but call it a "pen," *
And,—don't you see, then?—

---

* When Mr. Michael Davitt was on his trial at the Central Criminal Court, London, in July, 1870, on the charge of having been engaged in sending revolvers, etc., to Ireland, for criminal purposes, one of the witnesses called for the defence was a journalist and lecturer named Arthur Forrester. He was correspondent of the *Irishman*, and did all he could to shield Davitt. A letter was, however, produced, and put into his hand which threw a lurid light on the character of the prisoner, and which his friend and associate had to acknowledge was in Davitt's handwriting. The letter was as follows, the explanations, indicated by the brackets, being those given by Forrester:—

"MY DEAR FRIEND,—In reference to the other affair, I hope you will not take any part in carrying it out. If it is decided upon, and you receive Tim's and through him Fitz's consent, let it be done by all means; but one thing

Wid a stroke from its barrel their limbs they might splinter,
And not have to wait for the long nights of winter.
     And now boys, here goes !
     Which is Ayes ? which is Noes ?
Don't speak all at once, for it's rude ;
      But just whisper soft
      To the chairman aloft,
And your votes, if they're "Noes," he'll exclude.

you must remember, and that is, that you are of too much importance to your family [the Fenian organization] to be spared, even at the risk of allowing a rotten sheep to exist among the flock [the Fenians]. All care and trouble of the last twelve months will have been in vain. Whoever may be employed to do it [commit the murder] let him not use the pen [revolver] we have been selling, but a common one." (*See* Cox's *Criminal Cases*, vol. ii., p. 679; and *Times*, July 18, 19, and 20, 1870.

The Munster Maid.

(With apologies to the shade of TOM MOORE.)

THE Munster maid to the wars has gone,—
    Mick Davitt's voice awoke her;
Her porridge-pot she has girded on,
    And grasped the family poker.
" Munster men ! " cried that Amazon bould,
    " Tho' all the world defied ye,
This arm for you the fort would hould,
    These faithful petticoats hide ye."

The battle raged, but the foemen fled,
    Before her bilin' courage,
For first with her poker she'd open a head,
    And then pour in hot porridge ;
Till the boys from her petticoat folds crept out,
    And accepted her invitation,
To help her to finish the stirabout,
    On an inward application.

Willy, I Hardly Knew You.

As I tuk the road to College Green,
        Hurroo! Hurroo!
As I tuk the road to College Green,
        Hurroo! Hurroo!
As I tuk the road to College Green,
Wid my twirlin' stick and my cocked caubeen,
Says Erin, " The likes was never seen ;
        Willy, I hardly knew you!
        Wid your green turned coat
        Buttoned up to your throat,
'Tis the divil's delight to view you.
O darlin' dear, you look so queer,
        Faith, Willy, I hardly knew you.

" Where are your eyes that flashed so dread ?
        Hurroo! Hurroo!
Where are your eyes that flashed so dread ?
        Hurroo! Hurroo!
Where are your eyes that flashed so dread,
That I thought on the spot they'd strike me dead ?
Faith! they're smilin' upon me now instead ;

"Oh darlin' dear, you look so queer,
Faith, Willy, I hardly knew you."

Why, Willy, I hardly knew you!
    Wid your green turned coat
    Buttoned up to your throat,
Tis the divil's delight to view you.
O darlin' dear, you look so queer,
    Faith, Willy, I hardly knew you.

" Where is your tongue that spake so fierce ?
    Hurroo ! Hurroo !
Where is your tongue that spake so fierce ?
    Hurroo ! Hurroo !
Where is your tongue that spake so fierce,
That I thought my very vitals 'twould pierce ?
Troth ! it's now for Home Rule, wid its carte and tierce ;
    Why, Willy, I hardly knew you!
    Wid your green turned coat
    Buttoned up to your throat,
'Tis the divil's delight to view you.
O darlin' dear, you look so queer,
    Faith, Willy, I hardly knew you.

It grieved my heart to hear you rail,
    Hurroo ! Hurroo !
And pack all my patriot sons to gaol,
    Hurroo ! Hurroo !
But now, since so finely you've trimmed your sail,
And giv'n the Coercionist crew leg-bail,
Like a cod you're doubled up, head and tail ; .

Faith, Willy, I hardly knew you!
      Wid your green turned coat
      Buttoned up to the throat,
'Tis the divil's delight to view you.
O darlin' dear, you look so queer,
      Faith, Willy, I hardly knew you.

" I'm happy to see you've changed your tack,
      Hurroo! Hurroo!
I'm happy to see you've changed your tack,
      Hurroo! Hurroo!
I'm happy to see you've changed your tack,
And taken ould Ireland on your back,
And let ould England go all to rack ;
      Faith, Willy, I hardly knew you!
      Wid your green turned coat
      Buttoned up to your throat,
'Tis the divil's delight to view you.
O darlin' dear, you look so queer,
      Faith, Willy, I hardly knew you.

The Mudrake of Mallow.

(To the air of " THE RAKES OF MALLOW.")

WHEN the Landlords got the staggers,
Underneath our Home Rule daggers,
Prince of Parnell's carpet-baggers,
    Bill came in for Ulster.

Then he tuk a fine position
At St. Stephen's exhibition,
Till exchanged by extradition
    Far away from Ulster.

'Twasn't right of Misther Russell,
Wid such rude display of muscle,
Our poor patriot to hustle
    Out of Orange Ulster.

But you couldn't tame a lion
Wid the soul of Bill O'Brien,
So wid banners bravely flyin'
    He marched in for Mallow.

Dublin's best of rank and fashion
With his gallant goose-quill gashin,
Then across the ocean splashin',
    At one bound from Mallow.

Thinking Lansdowne he had snaffled,
But scarce rescued, bate and baffled
By his arm from lynch-law scaffold,
    Poor M.P. for Mallow.

Spouting, shouting to the Nations
Anti-English execrations,
Burnin' Royal Proclamations,
    Proud M.P. for Mallow.

Like the king of beasts his cage in,
For his stolen breeks stravagin',
Rampin', stampin', roarin', ragin',
    Mild M.P. for Mallow.

Yet O press your softest pedal,
For the martyr with his medal *
From the thumbscrew and the treadle,
    See! returns to Mallow.

---

* In the *Cork Herald* of January 27th, 1888, under the heading "A
Touching Souvenir" occurs the following description of a pendant presented
to Mr. William O'Brien, M.P., at a banquet on the previous evening :—"The
pendant is the shape of a natural heart, and about an inch in length, sur-
mounted by a miniature cross and surrounded by ten gold shots, intended for
reciting a decade of the rosary. Encased in this, and underneath a polished
domed crystal, are ten bullets taken from the bodies of the men shot at
Mitchelstown on the memorable 9th of Sept., 1887, where they assembled
to show sympathy with Mr. William O'Brien, who was the central figure at
the now famous trial of himself and Mr. Mandeville. The bullets are
amalgamated and rest under an enamelled shamrock formed of three hearts,
which are of flesh colour, and showing effectively a wound in each, as if

Like the radiant sun he's risen
From the dark night of his prison,
Balfour now shall waste and wizen
    At this blaze of Mallow.

See! around him how there presses,
With the prettiest addresses,
Widows young, ould maids and misses,
    Round the rake of Mallow.

Irish beauties are debatin',
English heiresses compatin'
Which of them shall now be tratin'
    Herself to Bill of Mallow.

Come! from out these charming witches
Choose one rollin' in her riches
To be your wife—p'raps wear your breeches,—
    My bould M.P. for Mallow!

pierced with a bullet. The three leaves formed of the hearts are supported
by a green stem, and are very striking. On the outside is a gold polished
plate on which is inscribed 'Remember Mitchelstown. Lead taken from the
bodies of Michael Lonergan, Jeremiah Casey, and Jeremiah Shinnick, who
were murdered by the police at Mitchelstown, September 9th, '87. R.I.P.'"

The Grand Ould Man.

CHRISTMAS, 1887.

*(To the tune of the "*SHAN VAN VOCHT.*")*

" I'm crossing o'er the say,"
     Says the Grand Ould Man ;
" For my Christmas holiday,"
     Says the Grand Ould Man ;
" But before I shlips away
   From Dover to Calais,
   Of coorse I'll have my say,"
     Says the Grand Ould Man.

" I'm going on the thramp,"
     Says the Grand Ould Man ;
" Wid ten postcards and a shtamp,"
     Says the Grand Ould Man ;
" I'm going on the thramp,
   Wid my hatchet and my gamp,
   By the light of Freedom's lamp,"
     Says the Grand Ould Man.

" I'm going to see the Czar,"
     Says the Grand Ould Man ;
" Lord Randolph's plots to mar,"
     Says the Grand Ould Man ;

' I'm going to see the Czar—
My only guiding star—
On an Irish jaunting car,"
  Says the Grand Ould Man.

" I'm going to read the lessons,"
  Says the Grand Ould Man ;
" The First and Second Lessons,"
  Says the Grand Ould Man ;
" To his Holiness the Pope ;
For I've consayved the hope
That he'll give ould Ireland rope,"
  Says the Grand Ould Man.

" I'm going to the Bastille,"
  Says the Grand Ould Man ;
" For a month widout appeal,"
  Says the Grand Ould Man ;
" And for fear my treach'rous foes
Should purloin my nether hose,
I'll wear a Highland kilt,"
  Says the Grand Ould Man.

" I'm going to Jasper Pyne,"
  Says the Grand Ould Man ;
" On his pinnacle divine,"
  Says the Grand Ould Man ;
" For I'm longing wonderfully
To be hoisted by a pulley
With that bould Milesian bully,"
  Says the Grand Ould Man.

           C

" Remember Mitchelstown ! "
    Says the Grand Ould Man ;
" Where they shot the pathriots down,"
    Says the Grand Ould Man ;
" Don't make the laste resistance,
  But keep them at a distance
  Wid *soft* stones and *tepid* wather,"
    Says the Grand Ould Man.

" And if your neighbour Teague,"
    Says the Grand Ould Man ;
" Goes conthrairy to the League,"
    Says the Grand Ould Man :
" *Don't* thrate him as a leper,
  Don't refuse to sell him pepper,
  But observe exclusive dealin',"
    Says the Grand Ould Man.

" I'm going to Chittagong,"
    Says the Grand Ould Man ;
" To avenge ould Ireland's wrong,"
    Says the Grand Ould Man ;
" I can't find it on the map,
  But I don't care one rap,
  For I'm *going* to Chittagong,"
    Says the Grand Ould Man.

" And from Chittagong to China,"
    Says the Grand Ould Man ;
" And Hong Kong to Carolina,"
    Says the Grand Ould Man ;

" At ivery railway station
  I'll explain the situation
  Till Ireland is a nation!"
          Says the Grand Ould Man.

" And when I've done my chopping,"
          Says the Grand Ould Man;
" My changing and my chopping,"
          Says the Grand Ould Man;
" I'm going landlord-popping
  With my dear friend, Colonel Dopping,—
  Of coorse wid empty rifles,"
          Says the Grand Ould Man.

" What colour shall we wear,
          You Grand Ould Man?
  What colour shall we wear,
          You Grand Ould Man?"
" Why, what colour should be seen
  But your own immortal green,—
  In the corner of our eyes?"
          Says the Grand Ould Man.

" And when will you come back,
          Our Grand Ould Man?
  Triumphant on your track,
          Our Grand Ould Man?"
' When Balfour's got the sack,
  And Salisbury's had to pack,
  Before our Paddy-whack,"
          Says the Grand Ould Man.

" And will Ireland then be free,
        You Grand Ould Man?
  And will Ireland then be free,
        You Grand Ould Man ? "
" Yes ; Ireland *shall* be free,
  From the Causeway to Kilkee—
  Then Hurrah ! Hurrah for ME."
        Shouts the Grand Ould Man.

Irish War Song.

(*To the air of* "O'Donnell Aboo.")

[Under the provisions of the Crimes Act a warrant for the arrest of Mr.
Jasper Douglas Pyne, M.P. for West Waterford, was issued early in November,
1887. To evade the service of the warrant, Mr. Pyne took refuge in a ruin
adjoining his ordinary residence, where, as *United Ireland* says, with "an
ample store of provisions and creature comforts, places of security, and
retreats in abundance," he spent several weeks in voluntary imprisonment.
When deputations from Tallow and elsewhere visited him, Mr. Pyne was let
down by a rope and pulley from a height of about eighty feet to within
fifteen feet of the ground. The special correspondent of *United Ireland*,
who visited Mr. Pyne, stated, that to climb the staircases, "amid a darkness
as intense as that of a railway tunnel, requires no ordinary agility, not to say
nerve ; for the steps have all but disappeared, and their places are filled with
loose stones which slip away beneath your feet. . . . Though Mr. Pyne
has a good many visitors to whom he speaks from his windows or invites to
brave the perils of an entrance into his castle, he spends, necessarily, a good
part of the twenty-four hours alone. ' Yet,' said he to me, with a smile, ' I
am never altogether without company, for I have two owls up there,' pointing
to an ivy-covered old turret, ' with whom I made acquaintance before I had
been very long here.' "—*United Ireland*, Nov. 25th, 1887.]

HAIL to the Emerald Hope of Lisfinny !
  " Honoured and blest be the evergreen Pyne ! "
Gems from Golconda, or gold from New Guinea,
  Pale by the glow of this jewel divine.
    Heaven, should his eyelids close,
    Watch o'er his nether hose,

Ne'er may he don the dread garments of blue :
      Long may his pulley swing,
      Long may he lurk and sing,
"Strike for Lisfinny and Jasper Aboo ! "

Ours is no clerk from a city or county bank,
      Blooming at Brighton on Bank holidays ;
Ours is a perfect political mountebank
      Dancing and prancing upon the trapèze.
            Safe widout bolt or lock,
            Scorning the peeler's knock,
Higher he clambers the more they pursue.
            Silence ! ye cynical,
            Pyne's on his pinnacle,
Blaze of our binnacle, Jasper Hurroo !

Then, as you'd witness a grand golden eagle
      Out of his eyrie high perched on the height,
Swooping to snatch the swift hare from the beagle,
      See our great Jasper darts down in his might.
            Hi ! Kern and gallowglass,
            Tallow lad, Tallow lass,
Jasper has dropped like a bolt from the blue :
            Pierce with your *pillalu*
            Kerry and Killaloe,
"Jasper, a Jasper, a Jasper Aboo ! "

There in the air like a child's coloured bladder,
      Softly he bobs for awhile by the wall ;
Then, like an angel on Jacob's own ladder,

"See our great Jasper darts down in his might."

Hark! his oration he fiercely lets fall.
    Never such fiery tropes,
    Metaphors, metascopes,
Blasted the coward coercionist crew :
    Scipio, Sosthenes,
    Burke and Demosthenes,
Pyne, were just poor penny whistles to you.

Well, when they'd printed your speech in the papers,
    Johnny Bright cursed you, you hit him so hard ;
Chamberlain over his codfish cut capers,
    Hartington fainted in Parliament Yard.
      " Seize him ! " black Balfour said,
      Cowering with conscious dread ;
" Fetch me that villain's head quick, some of you.'
      Yet still you faced your foes,
      Smiling mid owls and crows,
Wid your thumb on your nose, Jasper Aboo!

Talk of the sieges of Carthage, Jerusalem,
    Nineveh, Ascalon, Acre, and Troy:—
Had the blockaders a Pyne to bamboozle 'em,
    Plague them and all their manœuvres destroy ?
      No! your Psammeticus,
      Pompey, Leviticus,
Each had ten thousand of troops to subdue :
      Where's the comparison ?
      Here the whole garrison
Solely consisted of Jasper Aboo !

Lo! in his castle unconquered, our hero
  Bothered and baffled base Balfour's brigade;
Till, when their spirits had sunk down to zero,
  They just pertinded to raise their blockade.
    "Ah, would you wheedle us?"
    Chuckled our Dædalus;
"Come, of your tricks this is worth any two."
    So, o'er their cordon ring,
    Wid a surprising spring,
Safe on his pulley went Jasper Aboo!

'Where are you going to, Jasper, our Jasper?"
  His comrades cried out to that bould aërolite.
"To prepare Misther Speaker a regular rasper,"
  Says he, "on the very next Parliament night.
    For from my place, boys,
    Into his face, boys,
Like any flamingo by Jingo I'll fly;
    Until I have fully
    Convinced the ould bully
That though I'm suspinded I'll spake till I die!

The Wearing of the Blue.

O GLADDY dear, the prospect here's emphatically *blank*,
Since Balfour, that un-canny Scot, has laid me on the plank ;
I can't defy the Speaker, or insult the Tory crew,
But I pine alone, Och ollagone ! in a shoddy suit of blue.
I'm not a dapper dandy, but I've got a tender hide,
And the touch of stuff that's harsh or rough I never could
    abide ;
We're the most disthressful martyrs that have felt the Saxon
    scourge,
For they're tickling us to death in scores wid their sacrilagious
    serge !

Och, Gladdy, if you've any friends who serve in the Marines,
Be sure and tell them something of these awful prison
    scenes,—
How *minus* breeks for three long weeks I fasted on the flure,
Because they made me take a bath, a thing I can't endure.
Och, Erin, what'll come to you if 'neath his iron wrist
We're all to be blue-moulded by the vile ventriloquist ?
Dear Gladdy, if you love me, can't you snuggle down the
    flue
A suit of *any* colour but this everlasting blue ?

Oh, if the colour we must wear is cruel Balfour's blue,
Let it remind us that our blood's of that patrician hue!
Then pluck the shamrock from your hat and pitch it on the
    floor,
One day 'twill blossom in a brew of Kensingtonian Gore!
When Fraud's no longer lucrative in either of these isles,
When England learns to steel her heart 'gainst blubbering
    crocodiles,
Then in some other colour I'll triumphantly emerge,
But till that day I'll wrap my clay in sacrificial serge.

The Tail-less Fox.

" BROTHER foxes, in a trap
　　I allowed my tail go snap,
For I found it, by experience,
　　Most mischeevious to a chap.

" Let me use my battle-axe
　　On the brushes at your backs ;
And they'll be no more temptation
　　To the low fox-hunting packs."

So an ould fox made remark,
　　From his earth at Hawarden Park ;—
He might as well have axed their tails
　　From the bastes in Noah's ark.

For up spake Johnny Bright,
　　That cute ould Quaker sprite :
" I'm not of your opinion, sir,
　　And I think I'll prove I'm right.

" Come, make the frank admission,
　　That you envy our condition,
And out of spite concealed, invite
　　Our caudal demolition.

" You desarve to lose your *head*,
　　For the life you've lately led ;
But Providence was marciful,
　　And took your tail instead."

Execration Ode.

(FROM THE BALFURIAD, A THRENODY IN THREE THROES.)

["The Coercion Act has now been for nearly three months in force, but it is only of late that Lanky-doodle Balfour has gone in for carrying out the first instalment of blundering brutality. . . . Even the imprisonment of our heroic leader, William O'Brien, has not brought what Balfour would swim in if he had a chance—blood ; for blood is all he desires."—*Dr. Tanner's Speech at Kilmurry, November 6th,* 1887.]

O LEAN, lackadaisical lizard,
　　Foul filcher of hats and of hose,
Till the comb from thy crest I have scissored,
　　May I ne'er breathe the balm of repose !
May the bitterest blast of the blizzard,
　　Green gosling, ferocious and fell,
Hurl thee cleft, and bereft of thy gizzard,
　　To the hearthstone of Hell !

O pasty-faced, pallid apostle
　　Of devilry, death, and deceit,
Who with calumnies coarse and colossal
　　Conspirest our cause to defeat ;
Blood-boltered, fanatical fossil,
　　In gore thou wouldst gleefully float,
Couldst thou wring like the neck of the throstle
　　Every Parnellite throat.

Base booby, belovèd of Boodle's,
    False shepherd of Salisbury's flock,
Crown Prince of contemptible poodles,
    Demi-devil of Satan's own stock,
O Nincompoop ! nullest of noodles,
    Fierce fiend with the fatuous face,
To the limbo of limp " lanky-doodles "
    Get thee gone in disgrace.

Long lamp-lighter, lorn of thy ladder
    Vile, voluptuous ventriloquist,
Thou art making us madder and madder,
    'Neath the gripe of thy finical fist.
Art thou deaf, thou detestable adder ?
    Hath thy hide no susceptible spot ?
Wilt thou prick the great Parnellite bladder,
    Thou saturnine Scot ?

Peace, peace ; the forked tongue of our foemen
    Commands not one adequate curse,
One sufficiently savage agnomen,
    To hiss o'er thy horrible hearse.
Yet may owls of uncanniest omen
    Croon coronachs over thy corse,
While I prance on thy prostrate abdomen,
    And howl myself hoarse.

The Irish Vote.

(With apologies to the author of " THE IRISH WIFE.*")*

I WOULD not swap my Irish vote
　For a sight of the blind old Chian bard ;
I would not swap my Irish vote,
　For the satrapy of Scotland Yard ;
For howsoe'er I trim and tack,
　My chance of power's not worth a groat,
Unless I pack behind my back
　An overwhelming Irish vote.

Oh, what would be this House to me,
　Now John and Joseph stand aloof,
Without the sounds of Celtic glee
　That nightly ring beneath its roof ?
I love the rich, melodious brogue
　That ripples from Tim Healy's throat ·
Oh, Tanner's a delightful rogue
　On whom I delicately dote.

My Irish vote is staunch as steel,
　It never disobeys its head,
It shows no charity to Peel,
　But it has fearless faith instead.

" I love the rich, melodious brogue
That ripples from Tim Healy's throat."

It groans, it interrupts, it boos,
  It mocks the cock, the billygoat;
Yet, when *I* rise, no cushat coos
  More softly than my Irish vote.

For Cromwell's crimes to weep I'm fain,
  Bodyke goes through me like a dart,
I've got Boyne Water on the brain,
  And Mitchelstown upon the heart.
I've bought a suit of Blarney tweed,
  And Blunt has lent me his top-coat;
Job's comforters no more I need,
  Enveloped in my Irish vote.

I would not give my Irish vote
  For Vanderbilt's portentous pile,
I'd yield, without one murm'ring note,
  A spring of everlasting ile.
In my salad days I was half a Tory,
  Then I stroked the old Coercion boat;
But now I shall book bang through to glory
  For the ticket I've took is the Irish vote.

The Corporation and the Cholera.

AN ECLOGUE.

FEVER AND CHOLERA AT MARSEILLES.

[The Dublin Corporation, like every other Board in the south and west of
Ireland which is chosen by the people, has degenerated into a mere debating
society. The time of the Council is taken up by the discussion of barren
political resolutions, while municipal business is neglected. As might be
expected, Dublin, though the most heavily taxed city in the United King-
dom, is one of the worst lighted, worst paved, and worst drained capitals
in the civilized world. The death-rate often exceeds 40 per 1,000. The
sewage of the city flows into the Liffey, a stream which runs almost dry
in summer; and if cholera were to take up its abode there, the mortality
amongst the shipping population on the Liffey would probably rival the death
roll in Marseilles Harbour a few years ago.]

Fever.   Welcome, messmate, welcome, pest!
            Welcome to my throbbing breast.
            [*They embrace.*]
            'Tis years since our last merry meeting.

Cholera. Fond pestilence, accept my greeting!

Fever.   [*Sniffing about.*]
            I never smelt so sweet a stink,
            Except upon the Liffey's brink.
            How old we grow! 'Twas years ago,
            And yet the mem'ry makes me glow.

Dear dirty Dublin's scented lanes,
With houses honeycombed by drains,
From Hell might tempt the very devil—
For though in brimstone he may revel,
In Dublin even common men
Breathe sulphuretted hydrogen.

Cholera. Oh yes, I love the Dublin fare,
Where slums lie close behind each square.
We always found some stagnant ditch
Close by the houses of the rich,
From which through crannies small we crept.
For second course, while mourners wept,
Habitually we discussed
A helping of the " Upper Crust."

Fever. If Dublin flesh-pots are the best,
Suppose we journey to the west?
Yes ; let's be off, or while we dream
They'll cleanse the Liffey's living stream.

Cholera. Nay, pretty pest, they will not cheat
Old friends of their long promised treat ;
The Council would not condescend to
(Far weightier matters they attend to)
Expend their precious time in thinking
Of means to stop a stream from stinking.
For patriots, it would be a crime
On sewers and drains to waste their time
Or look a trifle nearer home ;—
Till they convert the Pope of Rome,

And force him to withdraw his ban
Against boycótting and the "plan,"—
Till Mitchelstown's forgotten quite,
And bloody Balfour scotched outright,—
Sweet spawn, believe me, they'll not clean
The lethal Liffey's cesspool green.
Why, at this very hour that villain
Is striving hard to capture Dillon,
And that, of course, must claim attention
Before a Bill for smell prevention.
And after that's discussed, I'm told,
The freedom of their City old,
Enshrined in caskets all of gold,
To every convict will be sent—
And that will take from this till Lent.

Fever.   To-day the City fathers flocked
Into their Hall, and having locked
And barred the door, under their seal
They vowed, that till they got Repeal,
They won't be bothered with debates,
And won't devote the City rates
To quench a stench or quell a smell.

Cholera. Then, sweet disease, your doubts dispel
In France to-day we'll take our fling;
And in the summer or the spring,
To Dublin we our way will wing.

Both.   Here, then, we'll stay till Lent is passed
We'll keep our tit-bit for the last.

The Wild West Passage.

WITH our captain old we're still out in the cold,
In search of the Wild West Passage,
We sight no port, our prog's run short,
And we sigh for fresh steak and sassidge.

But our skipper, he is in boisterous glee
At a castaway cargo we've found,
A crazy hull, of ensilage full,
" For," says he, " 'tis a sign of dry ground."

" And this grand green food is best for the blood,
When it's touched with a taint of scurvy ;
And dash my wig, if Biggar's salt pig
Hasn't turned us all topsy-turvey.

" So we'll swallow the shamrock and lick the leek,
And oblivious of all their bristles,
We'll cram our cheek,—like an animal meek
I'll not mention—with Scotia's thistles."

So he prates and prates, but we've grown so sick
Of his constant diet of clover,
That if he goes on with his scurvy trick,
We shall go for our old sea-rover,

And set him free on the wild west sea,
　As free as the wind and the air;
Yes, set him afloat in his jolly boat,
　Chock full of his jolly green fare :

Where the goose and the gull in the tempest's lull
　Alone shall list to his lingo ;
Yes, we'll cut him adrift, and leave him to shift
　For himself, we will, by Jingo!

Two Sides of the Question.

I. HERS.—BILLY MACHREE.

(To the Air of "GILLE MACHREE.")

BILLY MACHREE,
Sit down by me,
My love for you no more I'll smother;
But hand in hand,
My hayro grand,
We'll fondle one another.

When I was poor
In power, to be sure
My charms you didn't at all discover:
But when I grew strong,
You didn't wait long,
To declare yourself my lover.
The Irish Church before you fell,
In spite of your foe's resistance:—
Says you, " Its fall from Clerkenwell wall
Was a measurable distance."

Says I, " Stuff, stuff!
That's not enough,
The tithes they wouldn't support a plover:
Can't you do more,
Bould Billy *astore*,

To prove yourself my lover ? "
So your supple fingers upon the clefs
    Of politics you laid, love,
And the glorious tune of the three good F's,
    To the landlords' grief you played, love.

    I might have said,
    "Since you've obeyed
Your Irish maid so very politely,
    For better or worse,
    For blessing or curse,
Take her hand in yours, sir, tightly."
    But then I thought, in our after lives
    You mightn't prove so compliant,
For Englishmen sometimes batter their wives
    When they turn out a taste defiant.

    And so I cried,
    "Before I'm your bride,
You must first provide such a settlement for me
    As will render me
    Independent, you see,
Should you ever forget to adore me.
    For through this plan,
    You Grand Ould Man,
Though I've hopes of love resplendent,
    If it turned to hate,
    We could separate,
And each live independent."

" I and my beautiful bride."

And so one day,
With courage gay,
You accepted my soft suggestion;
Dropped on your knees
With graceful ease,
And popped me the Home Rule Question.
I raised you gladly from the ground,
I hadn't the heart to tease you;
And *now* that in one bond we're bound,
Like a boa consthrictor I'll squeeze you.

II. HIS—A LEAP-YEAR MATCH.

WHEN that gay and hearty young Irish party
Was only sweet seventeen,
I thought her as pert and forward a flirt
As ever my eyes had seen,
And I scorned her fancies and snubbed her advances
With the dignity of a Dean.

But a sturdy sage in his green old age,
May well be allowed a mate;
We're no longer chicks, for she's eighty-six,
And I'm past seventy-eight,
And in leap-year season it's positive treason
To expect a spinster to wait!

So if she discloses her flame and proposes,
I'll wed her with absolute pride:
Nay, more, I'll importune the goddess Good Fortune
To permit us to sit side by side,
With hearts still unsundered, till we're both past one hundred,—
I and my beautiful bride.

Tbe Arabian Knight.

[It would not be difficult to devise an appropriate *agnomen* for Mr. Blunt. Taking into account his fondness for horseflesh and his enthusiasm for Islam, one might not inaptly declare him to be the Arabian Knight of the Home Rule party.—*Liberal Unionist.*]

O ARABIAN Knight!
    Do not quail, do not shrink,
For your friends are showing lashin's of fight, ·
    And slinging oceans of ink.
And Gladstone has told the Pope
    Of your sad and perilous plight ;
And the evening star is full of hope
    My Arabian Knight!
    My invincible Islamite !
Then do not whimper, do not mope,
For the sanguine star is full of hope,
    My impetuous Ishmaelite !

Yet why did you go
    And defy the police ?
You're delicate, we all of us know,
    And were ever a lover of peace.
Oh, it makes me shudder and wince
    To think of you, frail and slight,

Condemned to lodge at the State's expinse
　　For one innocent platform fight !
　　My Arabian Knight !
　　My Protean Parnellite !
To think of you, my invisible Prince,
Condemned to scour and scrub and rinse,
　　Morning and noon and night.

O Mussulman horde !
　　Say, where have ye fled ?
Why linger ye to draw the sword
　　In defence of so dear a head ?
Oh, it's getting beyond a joke,
　　And it's neither decent nor right
For India to crouch beneath her yoke,
　　My Arabian Knight !
　　My sophistical Stagirite !
To make no effort to break her yoke
When you're shut up, like a pig in a poke,
　　Or a beggarly Bedlamite.

Oh, it fills me with rage,
　　And racks me with dread,
To know you're fretting in your cage,
　　And well-nigh worn to a thread.
But though Balfour is " on the pounce,"
　　We'll knock from that craven kite
Every single ounce of brag and bounce,—
　　We will, my Arabian Knight !

My dauntless Adullamite!
Though gory Balfour may fume and flounce,
We'll empty him dry of his blatant bounce
    And silly Sassenach spite.

I could scale Galway gaol
    On a fox-hunting mare;
I'd willingly plank it, and dress in a blanket,
    And share your prison fare.
For one wingèd word from your lips
    Would put my sorrow to flight,
Would be worth a whole cartload of Cheshire chips,
    My Arabian Knight!
    My Turkish delight!
Would implant in my toes and finger tips,
The strength of a fleet of armoured ships,
    Or an acre of dynamite.

But the waves of Lough Swilly,
    And Liffey's swart tide,
Shall be turned into suet and skilly,
    And totally purified;
And Tanner and Walter Long
    Shall in brotherly love unite,
Ere you shall pardon base Balfour's wrong,
    My Arabian Knight!
    My Blatherumskite!
Yes, ere you shall pardon base Balfour's wrong,
Arábi shall chase the Queen to Hong Kong,
    And reign in the Isle of Wight.

Poor Blind Worms.

Poor blind worms!
Cease, cease your squirms;
And I'll teach you how to wriggle
On the cheapest terms.

Crawl to the light
Of your glow-worm bright,
And he'll lift his emerald lantern
In pity for your plight.

Poor blind moles!
Gather round your holes,
And to your Grand Ould Gineral
Attind wid all your souls.

When I give the sign
To your grovelling line;
In your works, like very Turks,
Mine and countermine.

Poor blind bats!
Naturals and flats;
Read your Irish history
Like Kilkenny cats.

Had I giv'n it study,
When my checks were ruddy ;
Its present page were pure and sage,
Instead of wild and bloody.

Yes ! I'm reading my Irish history
Till the tome with my tears is blistery,
And I'm *making* it too, though the end of the stew,
I own, is an awful mystery.

The League of the Screw.

(To the air of " THE MONKS OF THE SCREW.*")*

WHEN St. Parnell at first took his coat off,
    To found our new League of the Screw,
Says he, " Now attend, and make note of
    The good rules I've been framing for you.

" My children, tell truth—when evasion
    Won't prove an effective resource ;
And go on telling truth—till occasion
    Is served by a contrary course.

" Hold each Leaguer confessed as a brother,
    In the pure light of Liberty's lamp,
All the rest you'll regard as none other
    Than lepers outside of our camp.

" Then the women—you'll bless or bla'guard them,
    Spake them civil, or boo them as fools,
Kiss or kick them, caress them or card them,
    As they're faithful or false to our rules.

" Love the landlords as long as they're ready
    To remit you a rousin' per cent. ;
But if to their rights they are steady,
    Pay them out, why, by paying no rent.

" Don't shoot them, though! tisn't convanient,
 At present, at laste, to our cause;
A jury of course would be lanient,
 But those judges play Puck wid our laws.

" Now, children, these sacred instructions
 Just stick to as steady as stone,
And after the Divil's own ructions,
 Holy Ireland you'll have for your own."

"When St. Parnell at first took his coat off."

The Home Rule Balpha-bet.

(About forty of the following epithets are extracted from three successive issues of *United Ireland.*)

A   stands for Arrogant Aristocrat,
B. Bloody, Bomba, Base, Salisbury's Brat.
C   Cold, Calumnious, Cromwell the less,
D   Dastard, Despot, Denying redress.
E   's for Effeminate, Eager for lynching,
F   Frantic, Fraudulent, Feminine, Flinching.
G   's the Grotesque, Gory, Ghoulish, Garotter,
H   for such Hypocrites Hell should be Hotter.
I   stands for Idiot, Insulting *bosthoon,*
L   Lying, Low, Lily-livered poltroon.
M is the Murderer, Mean to the Marrow,
N   Namby-pamby, Nefarious, Narrow.
O   stands for Odious, Owl, Outrage-concocter,
P   Pilate, Priest-hunter, Pitiful, Proctor.
R   shows the Ruffian, Reviling the blameless,
S   Swindler, Sybarite, Shabby yet Shameless.
T   Tyrant, Torturer, Thief, Tiger-lily,
U   Unabashed though Unspeakably silly.
V   's the Vile Venomous Ventriloquist,
W 's the Wriggler and closes the list.

The Doppingstall.

A Lay of an Unloaded Rifle.

Through the wasted wilds of Ulster
　　Stalks an Ogre swart and tall,
And that Ogre's name is Dopping,
　　Colonel Dopping-Hepenstall.
Senegambia never suckled,—
　　Senegambia, Senegal,—
Nay nor Niger, such a tiger
　　As this Dopping-Hepenstall.

Long he led the British Legions
　　From Nebraska to Nepaul,
Cleaving with colossal claymore
　　Recreant Russ and gibbering Gaul;
Till remote Mongolian mothers
　　Lulled their infants' loudest squall,
Just by whispering, "Colonel Dopping,
　　Colonel Dopping-Hepenstall."

Nay, they say, the very vulture,
　　Stricken from the stars, would fall,
Lions in their lairs would languish,
　　Cattle madden in the kraal,

Monkeys utter, at safe distance,
　One continual caterwaul
At the awful apparition
　Of the Dopping-Hepenstall.

Worthily was he descended
　From the truculently tall,
Rebel-hater, Ninety-Eighter,
　" Walking-gallows " Hepenstall ;
For that Loyalist gigantic,
　Heedless of their squirm or squall,
·Scragged the rebels round his shoulders—
　Hence re-christened " *Hempen*-stall."

Now retired upon a pension
　Quite preposterously small,
With his vile heart black with venom,
　And his gizzard green with gall ;
Gun in hand, his every pocket
　Stuffed with powder, shot, and ball,
Through the woeful wilds of Ulster
　Prowled the Dopping-Hepenstall.

Till this sanguinary summons
　From the depths of Donegal,
As he mixed his seventeenth tumbler
　In the solemn evenfall,
Reached him :—" Wanted, with your rifle,
　These poor devils to appal.
All expenses paid.　From Balfour
　To Col. Dopping-Hepenstall."

Tossing off that seventeenth tumbler
　　At one mouthful, spoon and all,
Dopping bounded forth obedient
　　To the Bloody Balfour's call,
Till he burst amongst the Bobbies
　　Like a Samson or a Saul,
And they shouted " Hi! for Dopping,
　　Ho! for Dopping-Hepenstall."

Agile as the goat whose silken
　　Hair supplies the Cashmere shawl,
Light he leapt upon the summit
　　Of a rasping rubble wall,
Whilst unto the midmost marrow
　　Of the mob, like any awl,
Pierced these awe-inspiring accents
　　Of the Dopping-Hepenstall.

"To obliquity of vision
　　I have ever been a thrall,
Yet my eye, with fine precision,
　　Marks one man amongst you all.
I shall fire with aim unerring,
　　Fools! unless ye bate your brawl,
And disperse in thirty seconds ;"
　　Thus the Dopping-Hepenstall.

And because along his rifle,
　　Laid in rest athwart the wall,
Yea! because along the barrel
　　He so squinted at them all,

The Doppingstall.

That each thought himself the target
   Of the Colonel's cartridge ball,
Instantaneously they bolted
   From the Dopping-Hepenstall.

Yet one rebel, one small rebel,
   In the middle of the maul,
Shrieking forth in childish treble
   On the turf was seen to fall,
While the ruthless rifle pointed—
   Pointed at that patriot small
From the ruffian hands of Dopping,
   Dastard Dopping-Hepenstall.

Fathers, mothers, in your thousands
   Thronging this Historic Hall,
Picture to yourselves *your* children,
   Pretty tots that scarce can crawl,
Cowering at that squint-eyed Ogre,
   Aiming at them, one and all,—
And condemn, with execration,
   Colonel Dopping-Hepenstall.

   *   *   *   *   *

I am sorry, very sorry,
   That I cannot quite recall
All I raved about that rifle,
   Raved in yon Historic Hall ;
For I've this Attorney's letter
   Fresh from Messrs. Flint and Ball,
Acting on behalf of Dopping,
   Colonel Dopping-Hepenstall.

Let me see—Did I say "loaded,"
  Or "*un*loaded," after all ?
Did I use the terms "blank-cartridge,"
  " Ball," " ball-cartridge," " cartridge-ball ?'
If I didn't do, I clearly
  Meant to mean that Doppingstall
Didn't mean to point a loaded
  Rifle at that patriot small.

Oh confound that mad professor
  And his curst election brawl,
I'd give anything in reason
  He'd not mentioned it at all.
For this low Attorney's letter
  Must be met by my withdraw'l
Of the whole charge of that rifle
  Used by Dopping-Hepenstall.

*   *   *   *   *

P. S.—Since I wrote my answer,
  Eating Dopping's rifle-ball,
That ridiculous Romancer
  Stuart has telegraphed from Youghal :
" Colonel Dopping no descendant
  Of the Hempen-Hepenstall,
Very vital, only title,
  ' Colonel Dopping,' after all."

The Green Above the Red.

For centuries we've been splittin', just splittin' wid the
  spleen,
To see the gory Saxon Red above our sacred Green ;
But now we'll soon be splittin' with laughter loud instead,
To see the English Robber raise the Green above the Red.

" You're foolin' us, tomfoolin' us ! Such sight shall ne'er be
    seen.
  Shall Saxons strike their kingly Red before the crownless
    Green ?
  Oh ! if you're true, give here the clue unto that mystery
    dread,
  That runs the Green, the rebel Green, above the Royal
    Red."

Well, when to Parliament that year by Parnell long foreseen,
Great '85 sint eighty-six supporters of the Green,
We all grew dumb to hear this hum from Billy Gladstone's
  head—
His bonnet, I beg pardon, sir —" The Green above the
  Red."

"'Tis not," he cried, " the Irish votes I vally one *trancen* :
'Tis not that just to bate the Blue I'm bound to back the
　　Green.
Sincere repintance for the say of Irish blood we've shed,
Injuces me to elevate the Green above the Red.

" *Sure, 'twas for this Lord Edward died, and Wolfe Tone
　　sank serene,*
Because they could not bear to leave the Red above the Green.
*And 'twas for this that Owen fought, and Sarsfield nobly
　　bled,"*
And they were right and we were wrong.　Shame, shame
　　upon the Red !

" Oh, then, in penitence profound, our Caucus we'll convene,
To the cry of ' Down wid Westminster, and up wid College
　　Green ! '
And every human feelin' left, stamp down wid iron tread,
But that which spurs our souls to rear the Green above the
　　Red.

" I have visions, blessed visions, of a glorious reign of
　　Green,
With me and Mrs. Gladstone enthroned as King and
　　Queen,
Whence Unionist and Loyalist for ever shall have fled,
And Might be Right, and Black be White, with the Green
　　above the Red.

But now the strife begins anew, and though our darlin'
    Green
Is still in a minority, through thim Dissentients mean :
Come, brothers, come, for hark! that hum celestial in my
    head—
I mane my bonnet—bids me hoist the Green above the Red.

" The blackthorn's spinnin' in my fist, I've cocked my ould
    caubeen,
And here's my coat to trail agin in honour of the Green ;
One deathless Bill still holds the field, though all the rest
    are dead,
Then follow, follow, follow, for the Green above the Red ! "

What, You?

[I notice that Mr. William O'Brien has recently made a speech—I think at Birmingham—in which he stated that so great was his admiration for Lord Spencer's recent conduct, that he would think it no dishonour to blacken Lord Spencer's boots. It appears to be a law of Mr. William O'Brien's nature, that he must always be blackening something. It used to be Lord Spencer's character—it is now Lord Spencer's boots.—*Mr. Balfour's speech at Stalybridge, March 24th, 1888.*]

WHAT, you, who when he stood to strike
    An honest English blow,
Stabbed Spencer with your poisoned pike
    His fighting belt below ;—

What, you, who vitriol o'er him flung
    With virulent ferocity,
Have you, forsooth, at last found tongue
    To laud his generosity ?

From this, my friend, may we infer,
    That when occasion suits,
From blackening Balfour's character,
    You'll stoop to black *his* boots ?

ꟼaiꟷ ꟼatriots.

(Addressed to Mr. Gladstone by the Irish Farmer.)

[The devices resorted to by Irish patriots to make a living out of the present agitation are numberless.

Few are fortunate enough to be nominated Lord Mayor of Dublin, by Mr. Parnell, with a salary of £3,000 and extras. But many make nearly as handsome a living by trading on the Home Rule ticket. Doctors taking the *pledge* are elected to snug berths by Poor Law Guardians, and are driven rapidly into practice. Country solicitors find it a safe passport to business; while the Dublin lawyers, who manage the League funds, make a handsome living by promoting League law suits, and feeing themselves liberally out of the League funds.

The Nationalist press offers a fine field for employment for those who can write; Parliament for those who can talk; and as for the rank and file, who can neither write nor talk, a breach of the law, followed by a month's imprisonment, is looked upon as a sufficient excuse for sending round the hat.]

ARRAH, Gladstone me darlint, me jewel, me hearty,
  For meself you've long leathered away like a brick,
Out of brotherly love, and a love of your party,
  And regard for yourself, Billy Gladstone avick!

You're the friend of the nation,—for tithes you've abolished,
  Disestablished a Church, and the Franchise bestowed,
The Protestant garrison almost demolished,
  Sure a bailiff is almost as rare as a toad!

You're the friend of the farmers, for now we have fixity,
  Rents below "Griffith's," and still in arrear, too,
Seed for half nothing—excuse our prolixity,
  Sir, and our humble petition give ear to.

Of course you're acquainted wid Mick—I mane Mister O'
  Flaherty, west there, from Ballyporeen :
Cato, Lord Salisbury, Sheridan, Cicero,
  By the side of our Micky weren't fit to be seen.

Wid his semaphors, tropes, alligators, skyrockets,
  He'd draw from the stream fish widout e'er a fly,
Or tears from their socket, or pounds from our pocket,
  Though the landlord and agent stood hungrily by.

He done us such sarvice in Tullamore cell, sir,
  That whin he came coaxin', we promised to bear
His expinses in London—that bottomless well, sir,
  For swallying money—'twould make a Nun swear !

He *must* be a gintleman—that we are willing,—
  But the gintry's hotel bill is one pound a day !
His clothes, sir, by Moses ! they cost 50*s*. !
  His washing the rent of a parish would pay.

And this is the rayson yer honour we're troubling,
  For now that for mimbers and crimes we are taxed,
And poor rates and pólis our burthens are doubling,
  Why, what is there left when for dues we are axed ?

And, therefore, we venture most humbly to cherish
  A hope that your Lardship will help us to-day ;
You've abolished the Church—save us all from the parish,
  And from Goschen's fat surplus our delegates pay.

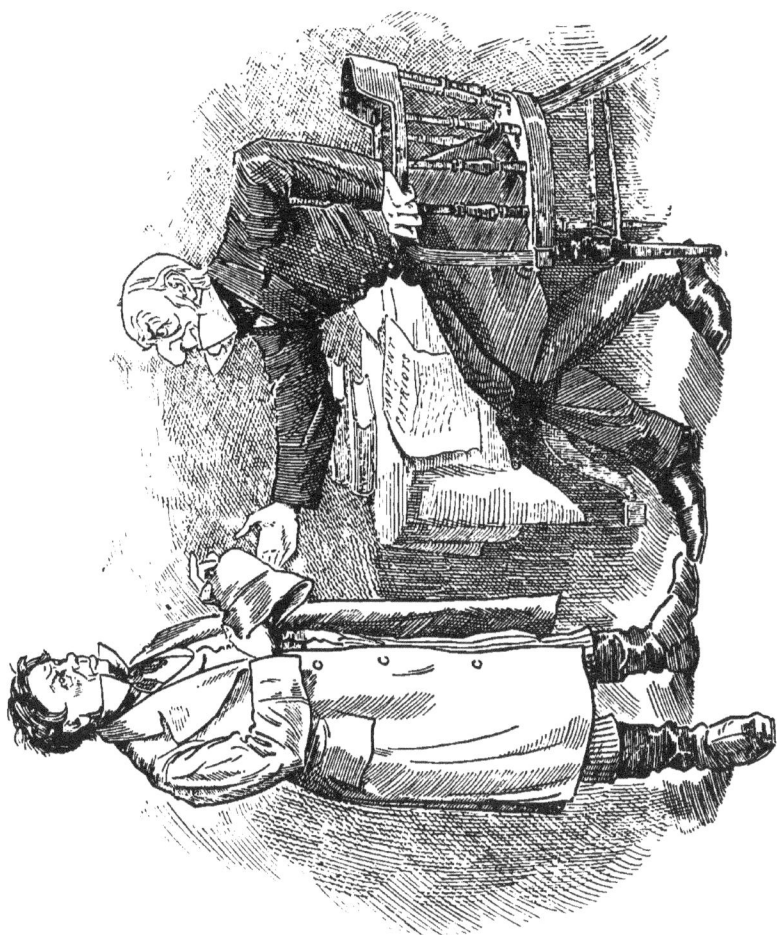

Cave! To the Classes.

VALENTINE'S DAY, 1888.

(To the tune of "BUMPERS, SQUIRE JONES.")

YE Englishmen all,
Who love to be shown all your sins by the score,
Attend to the call
Of one never frighted,
But greatly delighted
With "blood-guilty " war!
For I'm leadin' the masses
Agin the proud classes,
In a glorious crusade for Hibernian Home Rule;
And by the Lord Harry,
Wid thrust and wid parry,
Their strongholds I'll carry, or call me a fool.

Ye spoilt single men,
Who endeavour to kill half your time at the Clubs
Of the great Upper Ten,
And wid other men's wives
Waste the rest of your lives;
Leave your cues and your rubs,

And to gain true enjoyment
And honest employment,
Off, off wid your coats in the cause of Home Rule!
Quit Her Ladyship frigid
For bright, laughin' Brigid,
And iced hock for hot bumpers of " Whisky, my jew'l."

Ye poets of praise,—
First my lord, not contint that his brows should be bound
With the usual bays,
For his " kind heart " was set
On a gold " coronet"
Till wid that he was crowned ;
Then primrose-wreathed Austin,
And the fierce bard of Faustine,
Discontinue your satire so caustic and crule,
Or we'll boycott your lyrics,
And to drown your hysterics
Bid the Morrises tune up their harps for Home Rule.

Ye warriors so brave,
Who go harpin' all day on your beggarly pay;
Or so rabidly rave
On short and long service,
Till I'm growing quite nervous
Lest your brains should give way ;—
Swallow down your vexation,
And just take your station

CAVE! TO THE CLASSES.

Underneath my command on the side of Home Rule,
    And by all my seven sinses
    I'll promote you like princes
If you'll see me safe through this political dule.

    Ye clergy so wise,
Who problems profound can demónstrate so clearly,
    Come, open your eyes,
    And shut up your jaws
    From trajucin' our cause,
For this in your ear :
      " If without any failin'
      You'd wish to be scalin'
The steps to the throne of an Archbishop Jew'l,
    Like Archbishop Croke,
    Heaven's aid you'll invoke
On our marvellous mission of Celtic Home Rule.

    Ye pedagogues pompous,
And stiff college Dons from the Isis and Cam,
    Who from platforms would swamp us,
    Oh! you very deep, dull dogs,
    Oh! you classical bull-dogs,
You're not worth a Greek—*drachm.*
    But it's best to be civil,
    And if you must drivel,
Keep your drivelling dark in your chambers or school ;
      For continued transgression
      May mean supersession ;
So, good masters, good fellows, hands off from Home Rule !

Ye who worship the stocks,
Manufacturers, merchants, and traders galore,
        Whom, of course, it ne'er shocks
        To desave a poor body
        Wid shares or wid shoddy—
Is it *you* bar the door ?
        If I can't keep the people
        From England's church steeple,
Could *you* hope to escape, if upon the piled fuel
        Round your mansion or villa
        I should drop one *scintilla*
Of the mass-and-class fire I've aroused for Home Rule ?

        Stout squire and stout farmer,
That so long have been turning, in spite of his skill,
        Deaf ears to your charmer,
        I can't pipe you Fair-trade,
        But supposin' I played
On a land-relief quill,
        And a state-loan tremenjous
        Undertook for to lend yez,
Would you help me to mount the Prime Minister's stool,
        And once again follow
        Your grand ould Apollo,
Wid your throats and your votes on the road to Home Rule ?

        Ye lawyers profound,
Of your quirks and your quibbles we're sorely in need ;
        Arrah ! won't ye come round ?

You can prove black is white,
And defend wrong or right,
As you chance to be fee'd ;
You might prove green was red
To perfection instead,
And the land free as air, wid your arguments cool;
And bedad! ye'd be gainers,
For we'd give you retainers
By thousands, my friends, in the cause of Home Rule.

Historians and press-mates,
Messrs. Buckle and Dicey, and Lecky, and Froude,
And all my old mess-mates,
Before I salute ye
Wid my last *Et tu Brute*,
Can't we patch up our feud
Like the chiefs in the Iliad ?
Is there no balm in Gilead
To pour into the wounds of the people's poor tool ?
Not a ha'porth of whitewash
Historic, that might wash
This blackened soul clean from the stains of Home Rule ?

Ye fox-hunters bold,
That no longer can follow the horn and the hound,
But are out in the cold,
With no occupation,
Through this brave combination
Of the farmers around :

Come, leave off your sulking
For a poultry-fund hulking,
And game-laws that'll give you the sport of MacCool
'Pon my conscience I'll find you,
If I may remind you
Around me to rally
On your pig-skins, with Tally,
Tally ho, boys! for Gladstone, the Lord of Misrule!

The Irish Tanner.

(*With apologies to the author of* "THE SAXON SHILLING.")

[Sung at the inaugural banquet of the Gladstone-Tanner
Branch of the Gaelic Athletic Association.]

BRETHREN of our glorious branch,
  Though the blood-stained whippersnapper
Balfour, has locked up our staunch,
  Our devoted handicapper,
Tightly button up your fobs,
  Brand "No Rent" upon your banner;
Boycott Britain's brutal bobs,
  But circulate the Irish Tanner.

He's a leech of skill immense,
  He cures all ills that Erin's heir to;
With English sovereigns he'd dispense,
  Except in fees, and that I'll swear to.
He'd gladly crack ould England's crown,
  Then vivisect her or trepan her;
He'd do it, if he got her down,
  Our Æsculapian Irish Tanner.

Proud is his port, and smart his clothes,
  Most courtly is his conversation;
You never heard such florid oaths,
  Such ornamental objurgation.

Poor Peel he leads the divil's dance,—
    Faith such an illigant cancanner
Was never seen outside of France
    As our elastic Irish Tanner.

Into the jaws of Scotland Yard,
    Our Tanner gaily penetrated
Sent in his card and begged them hard
    That he might be incarcerated.
But no ! the gory ghoul in charge
    Refused him in the meanest manner ;
So still he circulates at large,
    Our own untrammelled Irish Tanner.

But " Tory Skunks "—for such is fame—
    Their savage onslaughts never slacken,
And strive, to their eternal shame,
    His fair and spotless name to blacken.
Envy always has a squint,
    When you're close enough to scan her ,
Sure, black and tan's a noble tint,
    But nobler far is black and Tanner !

The ould ship *Union's* in the slob,
    Her ancient Pilot's left the tiller ;
She'll fall an easy prey, begob,
    To such a desp'rate lady killer.
One lank, one lily-livered snob,
    Is all the crew that's left to man her ;
O joyous job, to wreck and rob,
    Behind our rampant Irish Tanner !

Waiting for the Tide.

(With apologies to the Author of "WAITING FOR THE MAY.")

Ah! my heart is weary waiting
    For the rising tide ;
Waiting till the wicked classes
Sink before the sacred masses,
As our Grand Old Man goes prating,
    Prating far and wide.
Ah! my heart is weary waiting
    For the rising tide.

Ah! my soul is sick with thinking
    On the rising tide ;
Thinking how to shun the utter
Horror of the Irish gutter,
Through whose hateful slime we're slinking
    With bespattered pride.
Ah! my soul is sick with thinking
    On the rising tide.

Ah! my heart is sore with sighing
    For the rising tide,
When our countrymen, who spurn us
Now as traitors, shall return us,

With our Home Rule banners flying
    O'er the country side.
Ah! my heart is sore with sighing
    For the rising tide.

Ah! my heart is wild with watching
    For the rising tide ;
Watching for one single lucid
Interval in the confusèd
Counsel, and bewildered botching
    Of our Grand Old Guide.
Ah! my heart in vain is watching
    For the rising tide.

Still I grope with groans disgusted
    For the rising tide,
While the herd of Tory scoffers
Smile to see our emptying coffers,
Grin to hear our banks have busted—
    Busted far and wide.
Emerald ass! why have I trusted
    To that rising tide!

"Oh, the Wild Charge he Made!"

FRAGMENTS OF A CONVERSATION IN A COUNTRY HOUSE,
COMMUNICATED BY MR. THOMAS EAVES.

["Three parts, and in many ways *the most interesting parts* politically, of the conversation have been left unpublished by me."—*Mr. Blunt's Letter, Times, March 26th,* 1888.]

". . . And when already wasted by tubercular com-
  plaints,
Their chiefs have gone to swell 'the sweet societies of
  saints,'
I'll run amuck from Malin Head to Ballinskelligs Bay,
Feasting my eyes with fire by night and massacre by day ;
I'll re-enact the penal laws, I'll resurrect the Pale,
And with your aid obliterate the Irish Bull wholesale.
Against the pig, 'the unclean beast,' I'll resolutely tilt,
And I'll force the population to adopt the Highland kilt.
I'll introduce the haggis, I'll abolish Irish stew,
And I'll scalp each rogue who dares to brogue or drink of
  mountain-dew.
I'll root the shamrock from the sod, I'll re-import the snake,
I'll raze the peaks from off the Reeks, and drain Killarney's
  lake.

I'll pulverize the Blarney Stone, I'll gouge out Ireland's Eye,
And ship the Giant's Causeway off to grace the Isle of Skye.
And when I've worked my wicked will, 'mid shrieks of
    ghoulish glee,
I'll blast the island from its base, I'll tow it out to sea;
And, acting on a hint I've had from crafty Mr. Goschen,
Appropriate the sinking fund to drown it in mid-ocean;
That Erin's exiles, homeward bound, across the surging
    main
For Innisfail's familiar shores, may look and look in vain."

"He has one voice as soft as the coo of a dove."

Mr. Orator D——.

(With apologies to the shade of Moore.)

MR. ORATOR D—— (now there's no use in guessing!)
  Like Janus of old has a double-faced head :
With one here in England he gives us his blessing,
  With the other in Ireland he wishes us dead.
        Oh! Mr. Orator D——
    One *face* is enough for a plain man like me.

He has one voice as soft as the coo of a dove,
  The other is harsh as the caw of a crow ;
The one mutters hatred, the other sings love,
  From *sol* up in *alt* to the D—— down below.
        Oh! Mr. Orator D——
    One *voice* is enough for a plain man like me.

In his falsetto voice he cries " Ireland a Nation ! "
  And then with his double tongue " No Separation!"
A Whig once on hearing the orator say,
  " I'm against Separation," cried " Which of you, pray ? "
        Oh! Mr. Orator D——
    One *country's* enough for a plain man like me.

Coming home late at night from a meeting proclaimed,
　　He was run into gaol, at the suit of the Queen,
And as the door shut, the last words he exclaimed,
　　Were " Gladstone for ever ! " and " God save the Green ! "
　　　　　　　Oh ! Mr. Orator D——
　　　　One *cry* is enough for a plain man like me.

And when he was tried, the Crimes Act for evading,
　　And for wearing the green on the Jubilee day ;
Said the Judge, " You shall wear, as you like masquerading,
　　" A new suit, for two months, but this time 'twill be *grey*."
　　　　　　　Oh ! Mr. Orator D——
　　　　One *suit* is enough for a poor man like me.

From his cold prison cell, so gloomy and bare,
　　" Help me out ! " he exclaimed, with a curse and a prayer.
" Help you out ! " cried John Bull, " Oh my ! what a pother !
　　Why there's *two* of you there, can't you help one
　　　　another ! "
　　　　　　　Oh ! Mr. Orator D——
　　　　Two months aren't enough for such martyrs as ye !

" The other is harsh as the caw of a crow."

The New Guy Fawkes.

I sing the doleful Thragedy,
  Guy Fawkes, the Prince of Sinisters,
Who once blew up the Parlymint,
  The king and all his ministers.
That is, he would have blown 'em up,
  For Guy had all the effronthery,
To sind each single mimber back,
  In that way to the Counthery.

He snaked into the dismal vault,
  At the witchin' time o' night, boys ;
Resolved to fire his divilish train
  Of Yankee dynamite, boys.
That is, he would have used that shtuff,
  And solely was previnted,
'Cos dynamite in James's time,
  Ye see, was not invinted.

But a little bird let dthrop a word,
  To James, that very sly fox,
So he had 'em search the aforesaid vault,
  And there they found poor Guy Fawkes.
A score or so of lively squibs
  Wor peepin' from his pockets,
And a Catherine wheel was round his ribs,
  And a brace of big sky-rockets.

But Serjeant Cox he collared him,
  Combustibles and all, sir,
And ran him clane away to quad,
  Right through Westminster Hall, sir.
That is, he *would* have done that deed
  Of gunpowder and glory,
But Cox, d'ye see, he didn't live
  Till the reign of Queen Victori'.

For thrial they committed Guy,
  Remandin' and remandin' him,
For more conclusive evidence,
  Till there wasn't any standin' 'em ;
And they'd not have found the missin' link
  They needed to convict him,
If he hadn't coughed the time-fuse up,
  That by swallying down he'd thricked 'em.

The Judge he sentenced him to death ;
  But they sent him a reprieve, sir,
And in two years' time they let Guy out,
  On a quiet ticket of leave, sir.
That is, they would have done all this·
  Some three odd centuries later,
But, as it was, they wint and tuk,
  And hung him for a thraitor.

The Promise-Breaches.

(To the air of " Purty Molly Brallaghan.*")*

Ah, now did you never hear of handsome Bill O'Brien,
  ma'am?
Troth, since I lost him, it's like a storm I'm sighin', ma'am ;
Not a lad in the land his place for me's supplyin', ma'am,—
    Ah, how could he lave me all alone for to die?
The hole where my heart was ye might aisy rowl a turnip in,
For he's tuk it right away and forgotten to send it back agin,
And widout it how'll I ever have a lodgin' to let for single
    men,
    In my poor empty bosom, till the hour that I die?

Well I remember as I read from the weekly *Freeman*, ma'am,
Wid my feet on the fender, I allamost started screamin',
    ma'am,
To find that Misther Balfour, that blood-stained English
    demon, ma'am,
    Had taken Billy's clothes away and left him in gaol to die.
Though 'twas November weather, I cut up my best warm
    petticoat,
To make my poor imprisoned love a waistcoat and a pretty
    coat,
And a pair of—savin' your presence!—lovely breeches his
    woes to mitigate,—
    Oh, after that, to lave me alone for to die!

By Parcel Post I sent them him through a turnkey friend at
 Tullamore,
Who smuggled them successfully to Billy under the bolted
 door,
And I got a halfpenny postcard in acknowledgment, and
 nothing more,
  But never since that day on Bill have I even sot my eye.
You know it's Leap Year, and they say there's scarcely a
 spinster, ma'am,
But is poppin' him the question from Lanark away to Lein-
 ster, ma'am,
And there isn't a wealthy widow but would wed wid him at
 Westminster, ma'am,
  And wid all that competition, what sort of a chance
  have I ?
Off wid my tale to Archbishop Croke himself I ran,
And then I consulted wid ex-Lord Mayor T. D. Sullivan,
He tould me *promise-breaches* had been ever since the world
 began,
  Now I had but the one pair, and they're walkin' on my
  boy !
Arrah ! what could he mane ma'am ? or what would you
 advise me to ?
Must my Blarney bags to Billy go ?   In troth I'm bothered
 what to do,—
I can't afford to lose both my heart and my breeches too.
  Yet what does it matter, when I only care to die ?

"Handsome Bill O'Brien."

An Irish Merry-go-round.

(To the Tune of " COME, FOLLOW.*")*

" COME, follow, follow, follow, to the hustings follow me!"
" Why should we follow, follow, follow, why to the hustings follow ye?"
" To bate the Blue and Green together with our Grand Majoritee."

" Come, swallow, swallow, swallow my Mudlothian speech wid me!"
" Why should we swallow, swallow, swallow your Mudlothian speech wid ye?"
" 'Cos the Blue and Green have bate us, don't you, don't you, don't you see?"

" Come, holloa, holloa, holloa at the hustings, boys, wid me!"
" What shall we holloa, holloa, holloa, at the hustings, sure, wid ye?"
" England's need is Ireland freed, as every man of sense can see!"

" Come, compatriots, come and wallow, wallow fast and loose wid me!"
" Where shall we wallow, where shall we wallow, wallow fast and loose wid ye?"
" In the green immortal Mud-bath of the savoury Irish sea!"

"No! by Plutarch and Phaybus Apollo niver agin we'll
follow ye.

We *dishtinctly* refuse to holloa that shtuff about settin' Ould
Ireland free.

We decline wid contimpt our pledges to swallow, and to
Misther Parnell to bend the knee.

And in your Mud-bath green to wallow we object, we object
teetotallee ;

For we've grown so giddy from your gyrations, 'gyrate by
yourself from this out' say we."

Let Erin Return to the Days of Old.

LET Erin return to the days of old,
  When she drew the sword—not the long bow;
Ere Malachi's matchless collar of gold
  Was collared by General Strongbow ;
And behind the brand-new presentation axe
  Of the pure-souled Prince of Hawarden,
Wipe out upon Ulster's fields of flax
  The stain of " The Cabbage Garden."

Till one of these days, as Saunderson strays,
  With his hands in his breeches' pockets,
He shall mark with amaze Belfast set ablaze—
  Set ablaze by our Congreve rockets ;
Confess that his ruffianly record is ripe,
  Look his last on Ulidia's fallows,
And one final joke put into our pipe
  As he climbs Kilmainham gallows.

" See this hempen article round my neck,
  Manufactured for tight-rope capers ;
Well, out of poor Saunderson's fortune's wreck,—
  Please copy this, Evening Papers—
An acre of arable land he devotes,
  And a dole of a thousand dollars,
For supplying the Home Rule Parliament's throats
  With these genuine Gladstone collars."

The Legacy.

WHENEVER I slip from this mortal scene,
  Oh, bear this gamp to my Morley dear ;
Tell him that lately I dyed it green,
  Of the liveliest hue, my heart to cheer.
Bid him not shed one tear of sorrow
  To sully its shoddy, so emerald bright ;
And no other umbrella to beg or borrow,
  Or mistake for his own, on a rainy night.

When upas trees I can fell no more,
  This ancient axe to St. Stephen's bear ;
Hang it up where I sat before,
  Like Damocles' sword, by a lock of my hair.
Then, should any Tory, when I'm in glory,
  Presume to reflect on its master's fame,
Let it fall, and slice from his shoulders gory
  The traitor's head, with one flash of flame !

Keep this pot, with a faith unswerving,
  To grace your revels when I'm at rest ;
It is full of the fruit, well worth preserving,
  Of a long, long life of labour blest.
Yet, leave it untouched, like the cobbler's bottle,
  As a warning of what I was and am ;
For Heaven preserve the tongue or throttle
  That tackles that old green Irish Jam !

"Oh, bear this gamp to my Morley dear."

Lines upon Lyin'.

(After SHERIDAN.)

BY AN M.P.

[*In confidence to his wife.*]

I TELL the truth while I am able ;
Still, I confess to many a fable.
But who, with Home Rule close in view,
Would lose it *for a lie or two ?*
Nay, do not curl your pretty lip,
Lies are the life of statesmanship.
When I'm in trouble, I deny
The facts, and say " It's all a lie."
If half my speeches were but true,
If what I swore that I would do,
I always stuck to, through and through,
The party's prospects would be blue.
No ! in strict confidence, believe,
For once I swear I'll not deceive—
When once the masses can descry
The difference 'twixt Truth and Lie,
Wisdom and folly, black and white,
Better and worse, and wrong and right ;

Then only, then, can Heaven decree
That I an honest man shall be.
And now, to make my meaning clear,
A whispered word, love, in your ear :—
While voters innocently find
My honied falsehoods to their mind ;
Or while they're false, and I am blind ;—
So long I hold my place secure,
And of my services they're sure :
But when each learns to scorn deceit,
They lose my aid, and I my seat.

The Anti-English Englishman.

FROM Polar seas to torrid climes,
　Where'er the trace of man is found,
What common feeling marks our kind,
　And sanctifies each spot of ground?
What virtue in the human heart
　The proudest tribute can command?
The dearest, purest, holiest, best,
　The lasting love of Fatherland. *

Then who is he who would deface
　The scutcheon of his country's fame?
Who calls each conquest a disgrace,
　Each victory the veriest shame?
One wretch alone on earth you'll meet,
　Though all the universe you scan,
So steeped in treason and deceit,—
　The Anti-English Englishman.

Where'er he goes he subtly sows
　The dragon-teeth of civil strife;
Each hidden smart with deadly art
　He probes anew to festering life.

---

* From Harkan's "Anti-Irish Irishman."

Were England stripped of power, and laid
   Beneath a universal ban,
He'd meet the prospect undismayed,—
   The Anti-English Englishman.

Where treason teems and hate is hot,
   He finds his true, his native soil,
And keeps the rank Rebellion-pot
   For ever on the over-boil.
What, with our deadliest foemen close,
   And charge triumphant in our van ?
He'd rather fly with England's foes,—
   The Anti-English Englishman.

'Tis his unnatural task to breach
   His country's walls and lay them low,
And then in rounded phrase to preach
   Submission to a savage foe.
Majuba's height was his delight,
   That peace-at-all-price partisan ;
He'd have us yield in every field,—
   The Anti-English Englishman.

The anarchist from o'er the wave
   Steered his fell bark to Erin's beach,
And, leagued•with every native knave,
   Preyed on her life-blood like a leech.
Who clasped that parricidal hand ?
   Who all the recreant crew outran ?
The blackest of that baneful band,—.
   The Anti-English Englishman.

Yet, Erin, hope! Thy tyrant's reign
  Is reeling at the righteous blast,
The monstrous shadows flee amain,
  The judgment day is dawning fast.
Oh! then shall Heav'n's high wrath consume
  With all his misbegotten clan,
O'erwhelmed in dark untimely doom,
  The Anti-English Englishman.

www.ingramcontent.com/pod-product-compliance
Lightning Source LLC
Chambersburg PA
CBHW030624270326
41927CB00007B/1298